Ice-Cream Cows and Mitten Sheep

by Jane Belk Moncure
illustrated by Joy Friedman

Published by  THE CHILD'S WORLD ®

Mankato, Minnesota

The Library — A Magic Castle

Come to the magic castle
When you are growing tall.
Rows upon rows of Word Windows
Line every single wall.
They reach up high,
As high as the sky,
And you want to open them all.
For every time you open one,
A new adventure has begun.

David opened a Word Window.
Guess what David saw?

Cows. Lots of cows.
"Hi, Cows," said David.
What did the cows say?

The cows were on their way to the
barn. So David went too.

"Hi," said a farmer. "You are just
in time. . .

to see me milk the cows."

"What will you do with the milk?"
asked David.

"A milk truck will come.
It will take the milk to. . .

the dairy where the milk
will be made into. . .

butter,

milk to drink,

ice cream,

cheese,   and   yogurt

for you," said the farmer.

David gave each cow a pat on the head.

"Thank-you, Cow," he said. "Thanks for all you do for me."

Then David saw sheep. . .

lots of sheep.

"Hi, Sheep," he said.
What did the sheep say?

The sheep were on their way to
the barn. So. . .

David went too.

"Hi," said a farmer. "You are just
in time to see me give. . .

haircuts
to my sheep."

Clip-clip. Clip-clip. Off came the
sheep's wool.

"What will you do with the wool?"
asked David.

"A truck will take the wool to the
woolen mill," said the farmer.

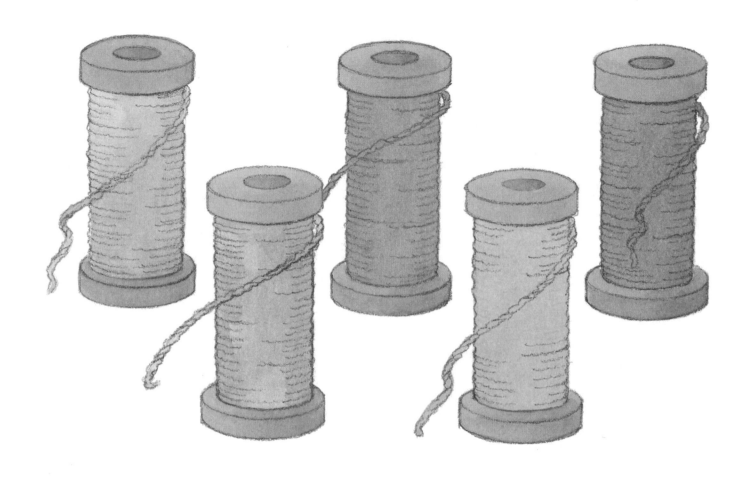

"At the mill, the wool will be made into yarn. All colors of yarn. Yarn for. . .

a sweater,

scarf,

slippers

and

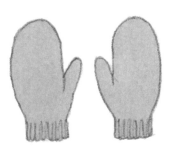

mittens

for you," said the farmer.

David gave each sheep a pat on the head.

"Thank-you, Sheep," he said. "Thanks for all you do for me."

Then the farmer took David to see his hens. "Hi, Hens," said David. What did the hens say?

The hens were on their way to the henhouse, so. . .

David went too. Guess what he found?

Eggs, lots of eggs. . . . Eggs to. . .

fry,

scramble,

boil,

and put in an
Easter basket.

What did David give each hen?
What did David say?

David wanted to stay at the farm,
but it was time to go home.

"Bye-bye, farm friends," said David.
"Bye-bye."

And David closed the Word Window.

When David went home, he made these pictures of farm-friends.
So can you.

milk

cheese

ice cream

cow

butter

yogurt